InBetween

The Unseen

Jessica Gorman

Vitek Kruta

Published by Human Error Publishing
www.humanerrorpublishing.com
paul@humanerrorpublishing.com

Copyright © 2025
by
Human Error Publishing
Jessica Gorman and Vitek Kruta

All Rights Reserved

ISBN: 978-1-948521-83-3

Cover Design: Jessica Gorman and Vitek Kruta

Human Error Publishing asks that no part of this publication be reproduced or transmitted in any form or by any means electronic or mechanical, including photocopy, recording or information storage or retrieval system without permission in writing from Jessica Gorman, Vitek Kruta and Human Error Publishing. The reasons for this are to help support the publisher and the artists.

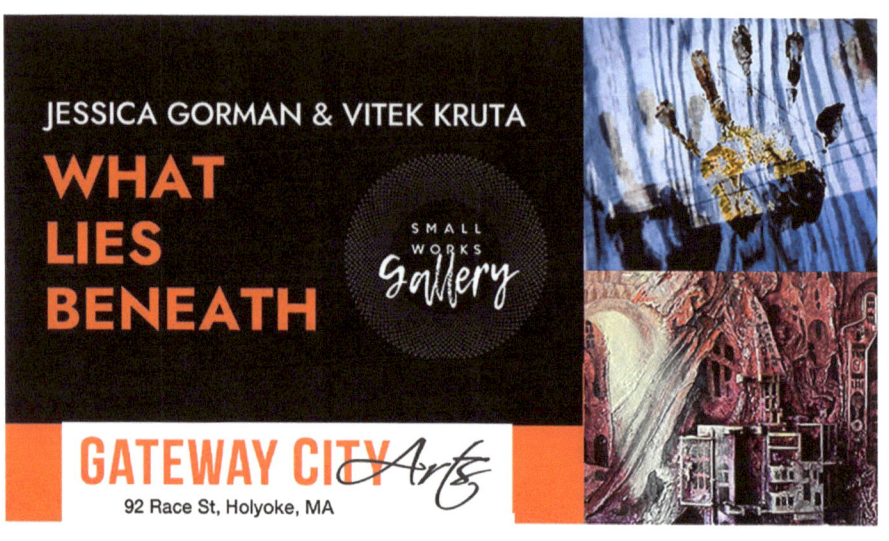

Table of Content

Jessica Gorman bio	6
Vitek Kruta bio	7
Vitek Kruta	9
DREAMS	11
UN-TROPY	13
INCONSEQUENTIALITY	15
CHANGE	17
NOA'S ARK'S DESTINATION ARARAT	19
WHAT LIES BENEATH	21
WHEN DID THE FISH DECIDE TO BE A GOLD FISH?	23
FROZEN IN TIME	25
JUST MOMENTS	27
Jessica Gorman	29
A SHADOW'S KEEP	31
WINDSWEPT DREAMS	33
CIRCLES UNSEEN	35
FEAR OF THE FALL; THRILL OF THE JUMP	37
ETERNAL SLEEP	39
A CHILD'S PLEA	41
A NIGHTMARE'S SCREAM	43
WHEN THE BLOSSOMS FREEZE	45
OUR FINAL BREATHS & TESTAMENTS	47
Review: In Between The Unseen	52

Jessica Gorman

is a lifelong artist and writer from the Holyoke area, and former employee and featured artist at Gateway City Arts until it's closing in 2024. After graduating from UMass Amherst studying Psychology, Jessica spent more than ten years working with adults and children struggling with mental illness and developmental challenges. Strongly impacted and inspired by these experiences, Jessica's works focus on the exploration and expressions of the inner self in its many forms as it navigates and evolves through the many stages of its being; and how universally felt obstacles such as grief, loss, fear, thought distortion and trauma uniquely shape that personal experience and influence how we perceive the world.

Jessica utilizes a variety of creative and alternative materials to shape the essence of her message into vivid interactive imagery through combinations of written word, abstract photography, and using "found" and recycled objects to create three dimensional and textured works of visual art on canvas

Jessica's work was recognized by the Deerfield Valley Art Association with several of her masks earning honorable mentions in the 2020 COVID Art Contest, and her multi-media canvas "For Those Who Died Alone" taking First place and Best in Show. Jessica's poetry, photography, and multimedia creations were displayed throughout the post Covid years at Gateway city arts before its closing in 2024. She continues to work privately as an artist in the area.

Vitek Kruta
(born in Prague, Czech Republic)

was trained in Old-World techniques of Fine and Decorative Arts in Czech Republic and Germany, where he attended schools and worked with master craftsman as restorer of paintings, murals frescoes, architectural elements, sculptures and painted furniture in historical buildings, castles and churches before coming to the United States in 1991.

Since his arrival to USA, Mr. Kruta continues his carrier as freelance artist, designer and art restorer, teacher, instructor and consultant for various public and not for profit organizations and groups, schools and business associates.

Inspired by his restoration experience and Old world artistic sensibility, Mr.Kruta developed unique style in which he created hundreds of distinct and original paintings and 3D mixed media works of art, which he exhibits in Galleries and Art shows trough out the country. Formal Member of American Craft Council and Paradise City Art Festivals and locally featured at Michelson Art Gallery in Northampton. His work has been featured in exhibitions in former Czechoslovakia, France, Germany, United States and Canada.

Mr. Kruta, is co-founder/director of Gateway City Arts.

Vitek Kruta

My inspiration for my painting comes from a lifelong fascination with world history and how it has been shaped—and reshaped—by humankind.In *BETWEEN THE UNSEEN*, hidden within countless layers, lie traces of human drama and ingenuity—evidence of survival and the endurance of our species. The remnants unearthed through archaeological digs, accidental discoveries, or natural disasters echo not only through the layers of the Earth but also through the deep layers of our subconscious. Psychology, like archaeology, uncovers fragments of our existence, revealing an incomplete picture of who we are, who we were, and who we imagine ourselves becoming as we move through the endless cycles of life—generation after generation. The complexity of consciousness—how our thoughts and ideas take physical form—often remains invisible to us, as if amnesia itself were a fundamental survival mechanism, allowing us to adapt to shifting paradigms and move through time.My paintings reflect the tension between the familiar and the mysterious, between what we know and what we cannot explain. This ambiguity often distorts our understanding of reality, giving rise to alternative ideologies, religious beliefs, and scientific pursuits. We build, we destroy, and we build again. Life continues—until it doesn't. In the end, only bones, seashells, ruins, and enigmatic artifacts remain to tell the story.

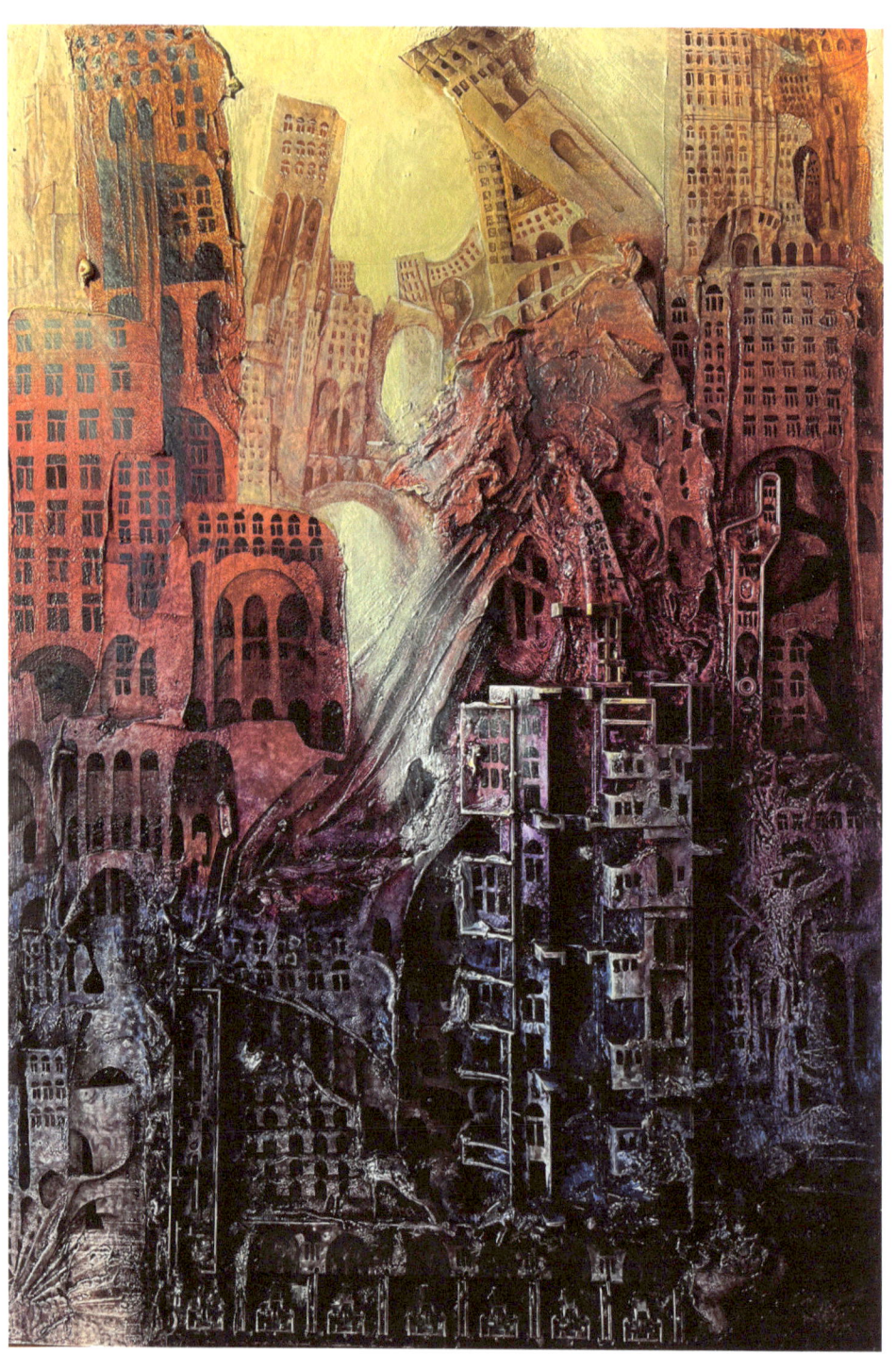

DREAMS

I have seen the end of the
world
many times...
...since the world ends for me
every time I go to sleep.
I travel far, far away in my
dreams
visiting a world
where earthquakes tear apart
the ground creating huge
scars in the face of the earth.
Where Tsunamis are so high
that make birds drown in the
sky.
Where giant mudslides
swallow cities and villages
leaving remnants of them
scattered like colorful
seaglass on the beach.

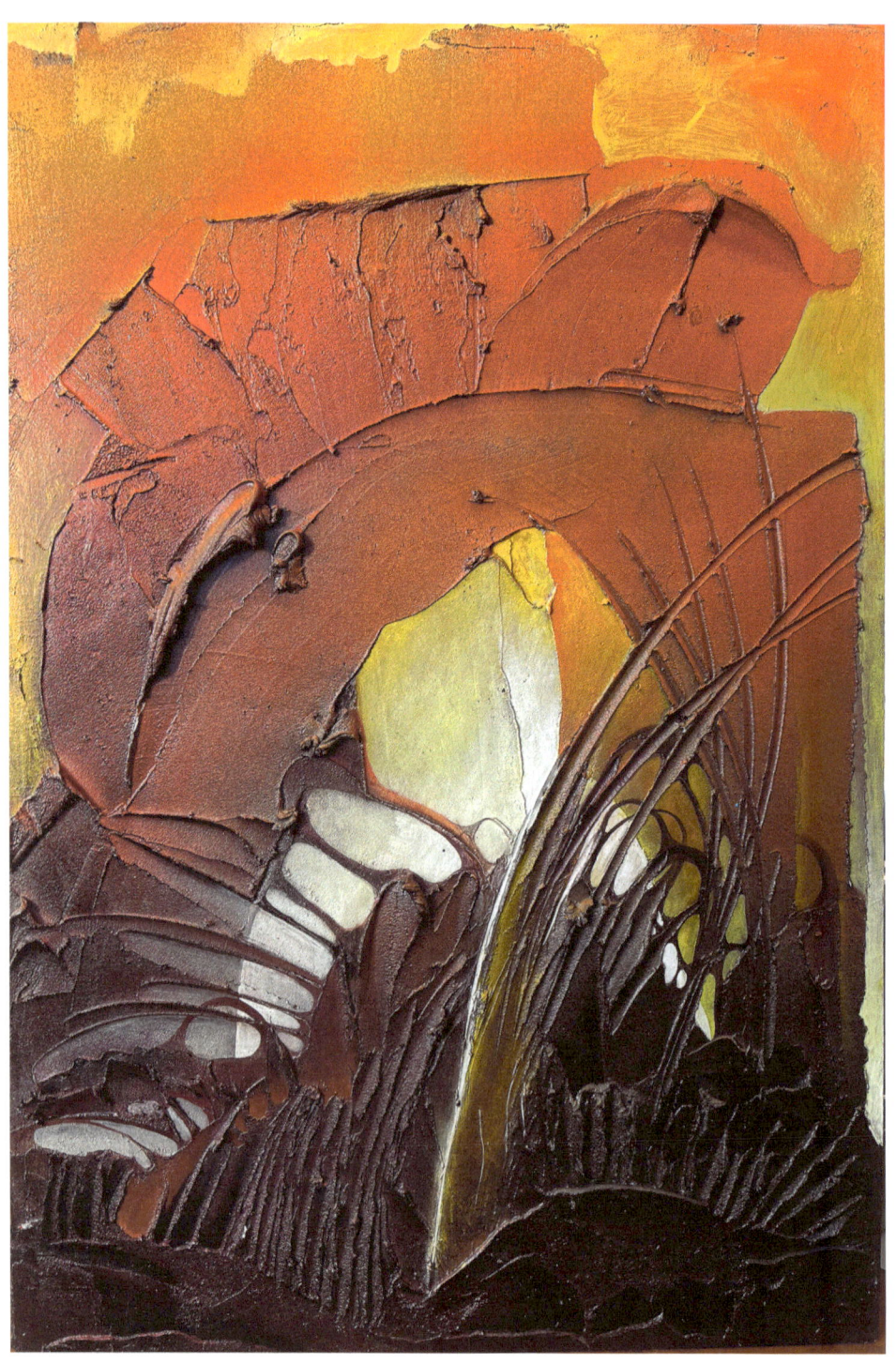

UN-TROPY

We come from chaos
and disorder,
thermodynamic quantity...

We represent the unavailability
of a system's thermal energy
needed for conversion into
mechanical work,
degree of disorder,
randomness.

Star dust perhaps
Chaos seemingly unorganized

yet beneath organized matter
and powerful order of unseen
and beautiful existing
relationships
on its own by themselves
harmoniously existing
not having to have to be
understood,
or touched by life.

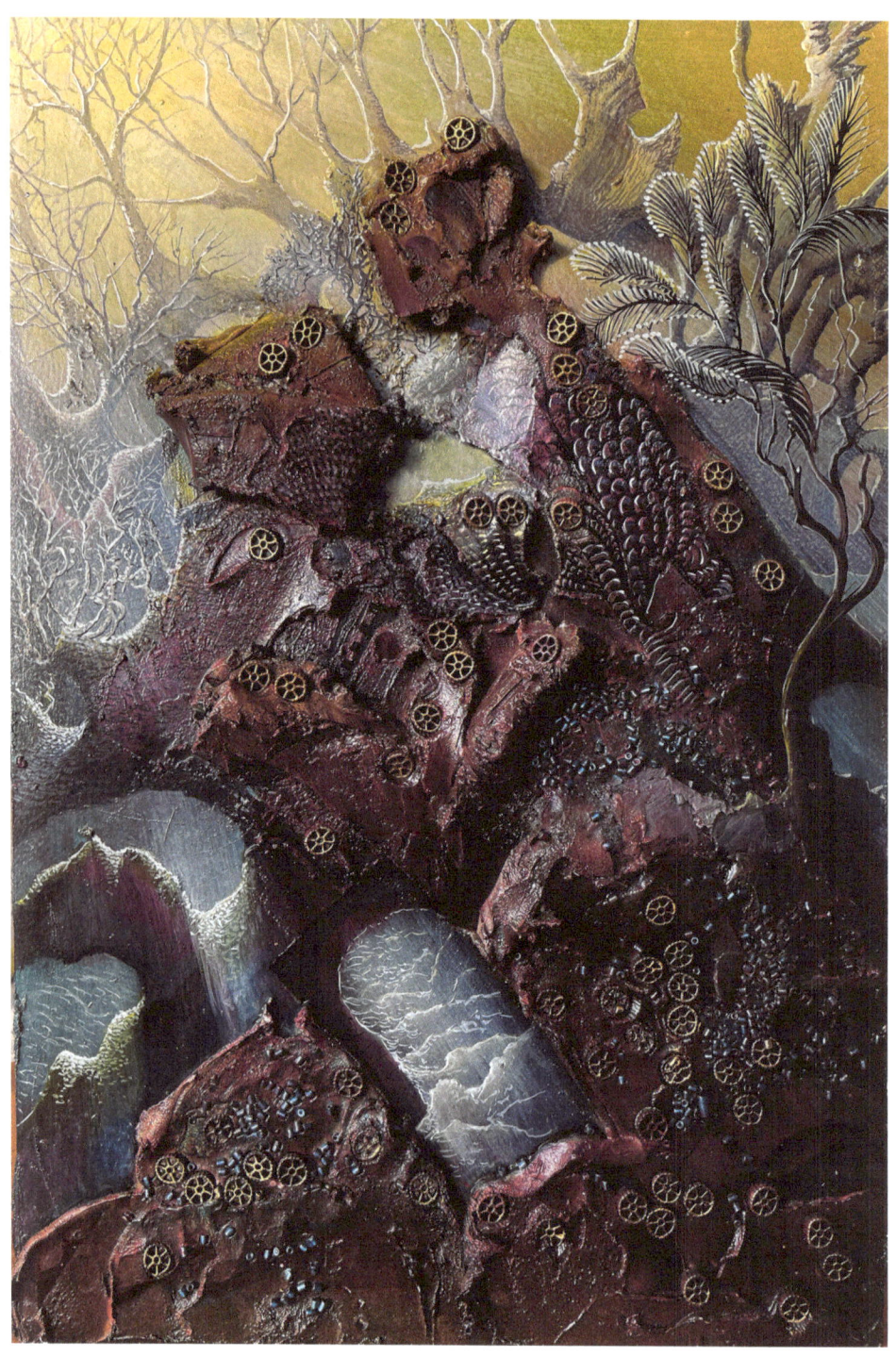

INCONSEQUENTIALITY

In water the word became
flesh
and on the ground, it turned
to dust.

Still waters
hardly ever reveal
what's way down bellow
at the bottom we can't touch
deep - away from light.

Deep is the well so is the
wisdom we share,
but shallow are the hands
that give away, what's left
behind or hold
what is yet to come.

And so, we wonder...
was It taken from us?
Or did we try to keep that,
which did not belong?
We forgot
as we pass through time.

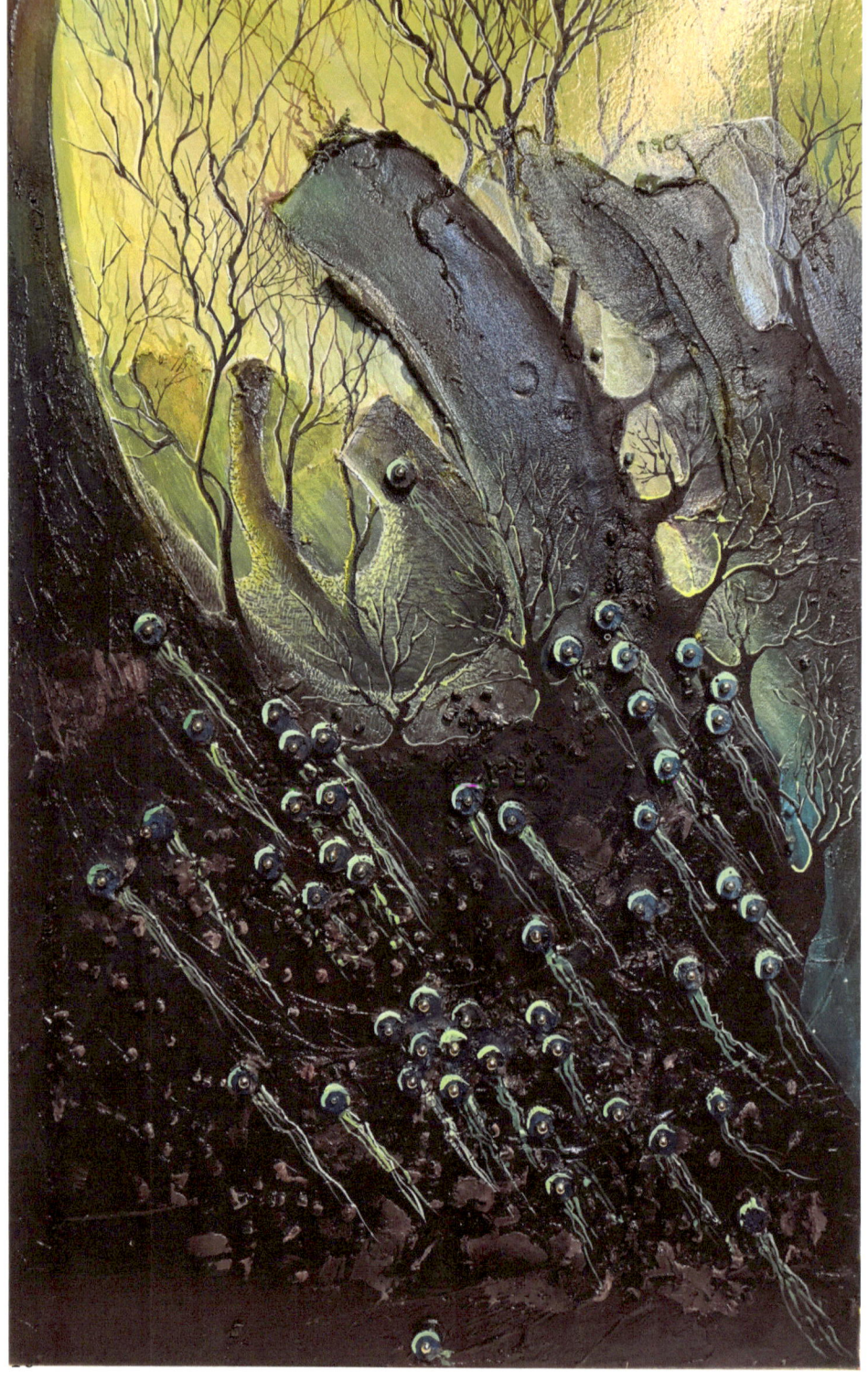

CHANGE

The safe and familiar world no
longer exists.
Orchards, fields and hills,
meandering rivers,
smell of honey in the air and
sound of butterfly wings.

The world I was hanging on to
was like a bird's nest
on the branch of a dying tree.
The world that made me
chase the sunsets
in hope to escape the
inevitable darkness of the
shadow...
absence of light......absence
of love.

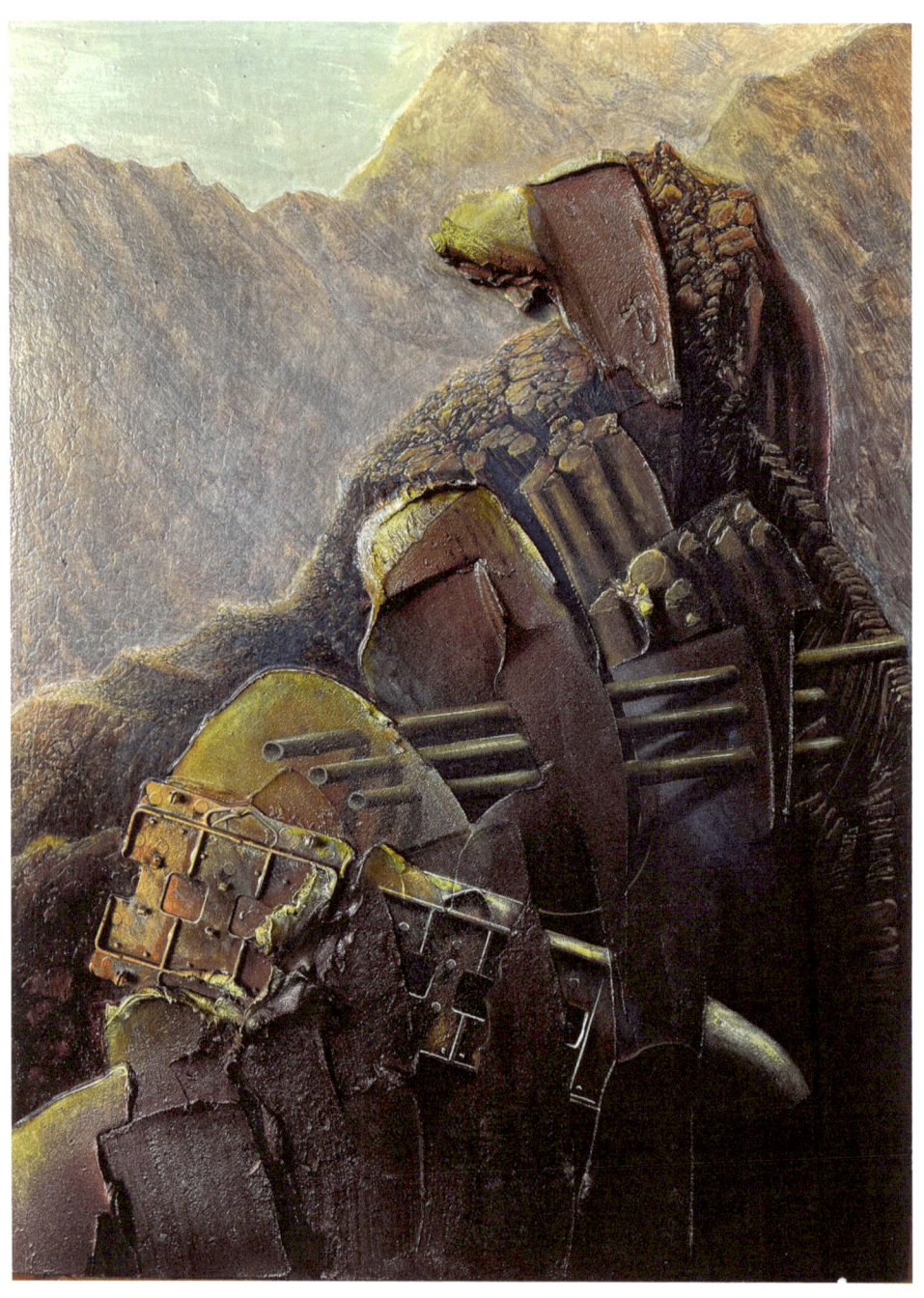

NOA'S ARK'S DESTINATION ARARAT

I spoke to the wind once, high atop a mountain, where even the echo of the world below could not climb, and no bird dared to rest on the jagged silence of that height.

Up there, where the sky feels close enough to touch, I let go of the noise, and the wind met me with open arms.

Time did not listen to the words we shared. They vanished into the thin air, unwritten, unheard—and yet, somehow, they touched places only the soul can feel. Only the wind remembers what was said that day.

And when I asked, "From here... where do I go? Which path is mine to walk?" The wind did not point, did not push— he only whispered, with a quiet smile in his breath: **"Let your wings grow and fly."** Since then, I have often spoken to the wind. He listens without judgment, answers without sound. And as I learn the art of flight— not with feathers, but with faith, not with motion, but with trust— he lifts me gently now and then, cradling me in his arms, reminding me that falling and flying are sometimes the same.

The wind has many things to say, but only to those who dare to climb high enough to hear what silence has been meaning to say all along.

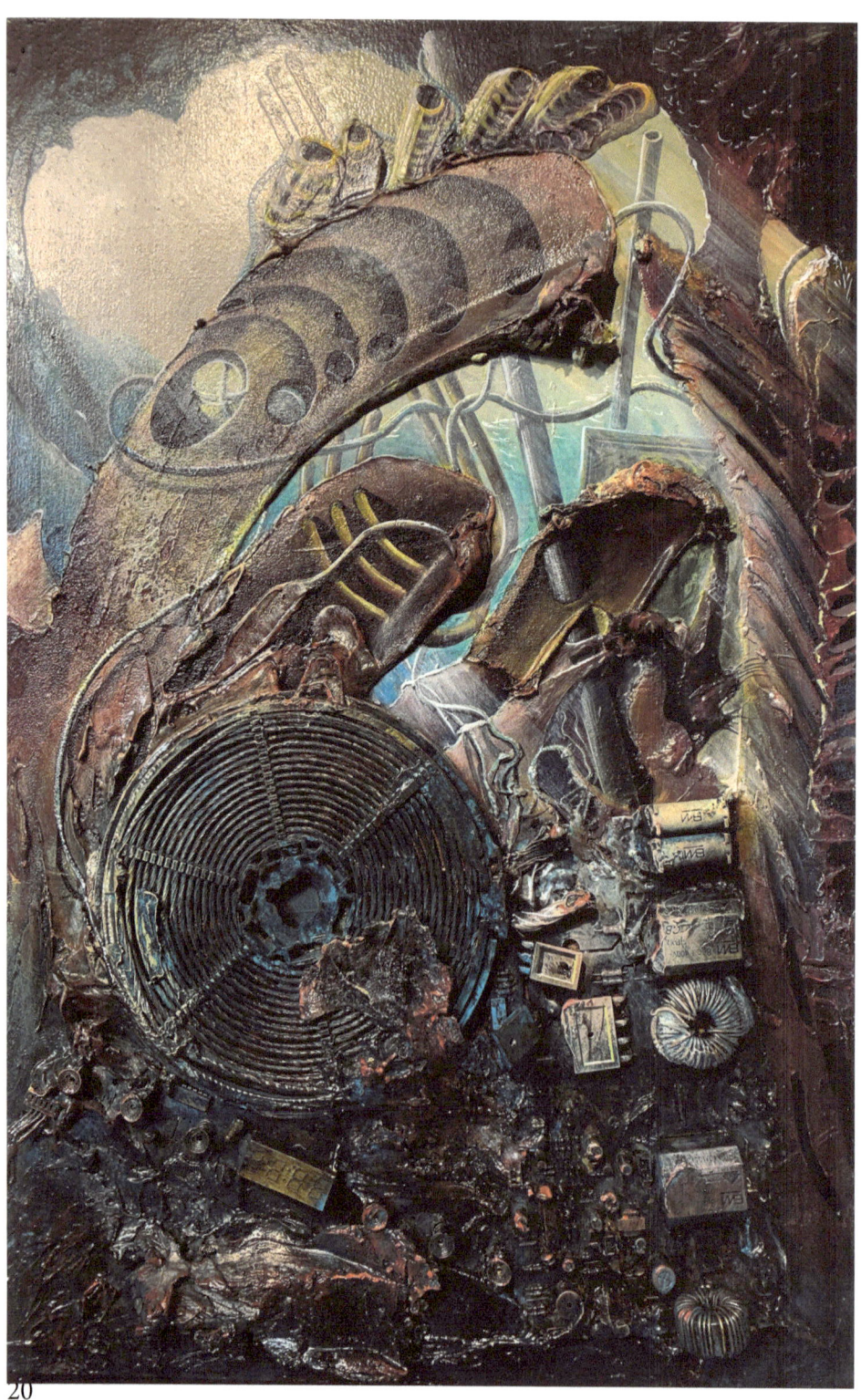

WHAT LIES BENEATH

In the darkness beneath
Shadow is absence of light
Like hate is absence of love
The magic lamp shines from within
A flame that's burning
in every heart touched by love

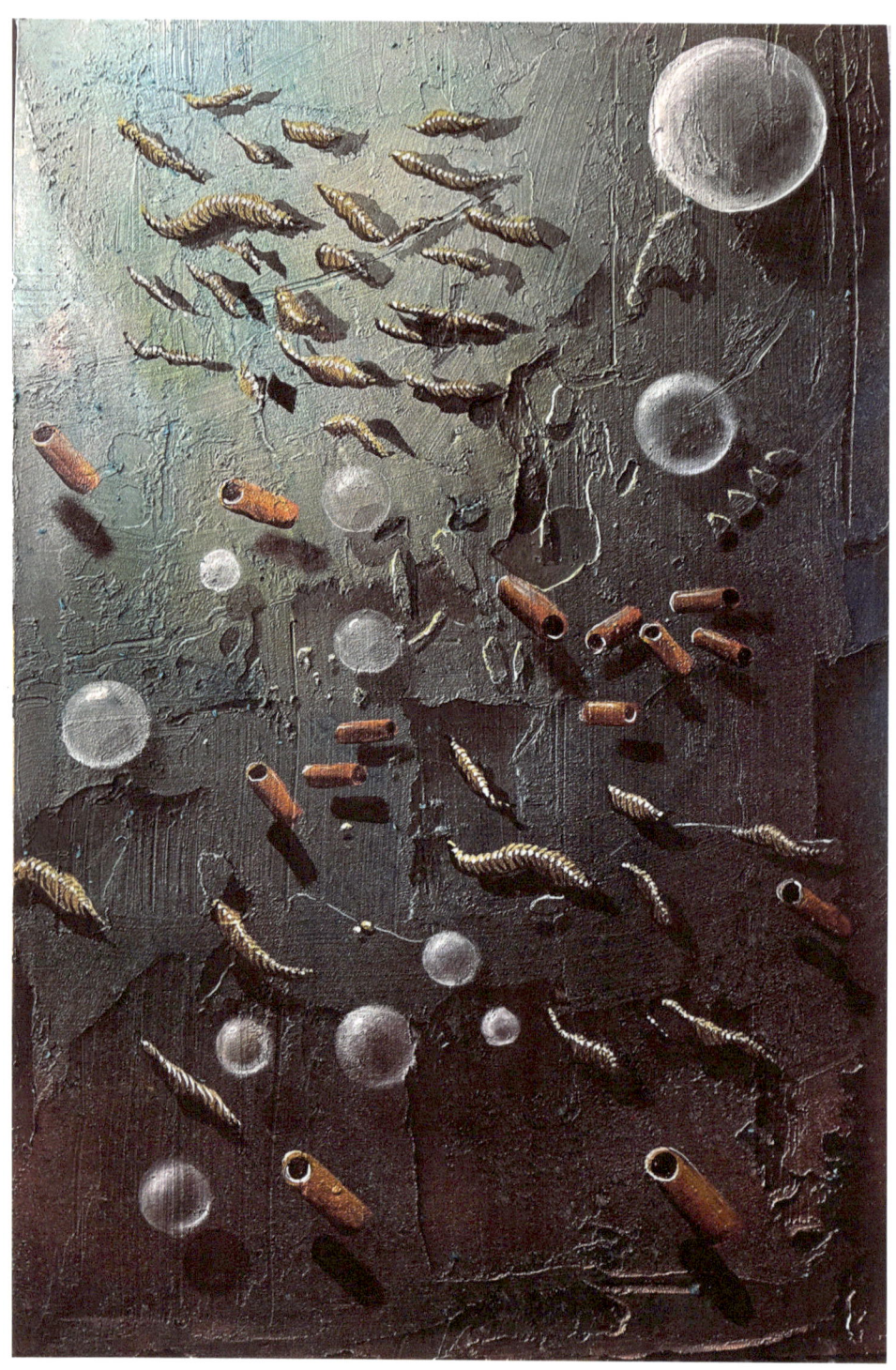

WHEN DID THE FISH DECIDE TO BE A GOLD FISH?

And let there be light....
and let there be life....
And let there be a gold Fish

And let it be
Just let it simply be..
please

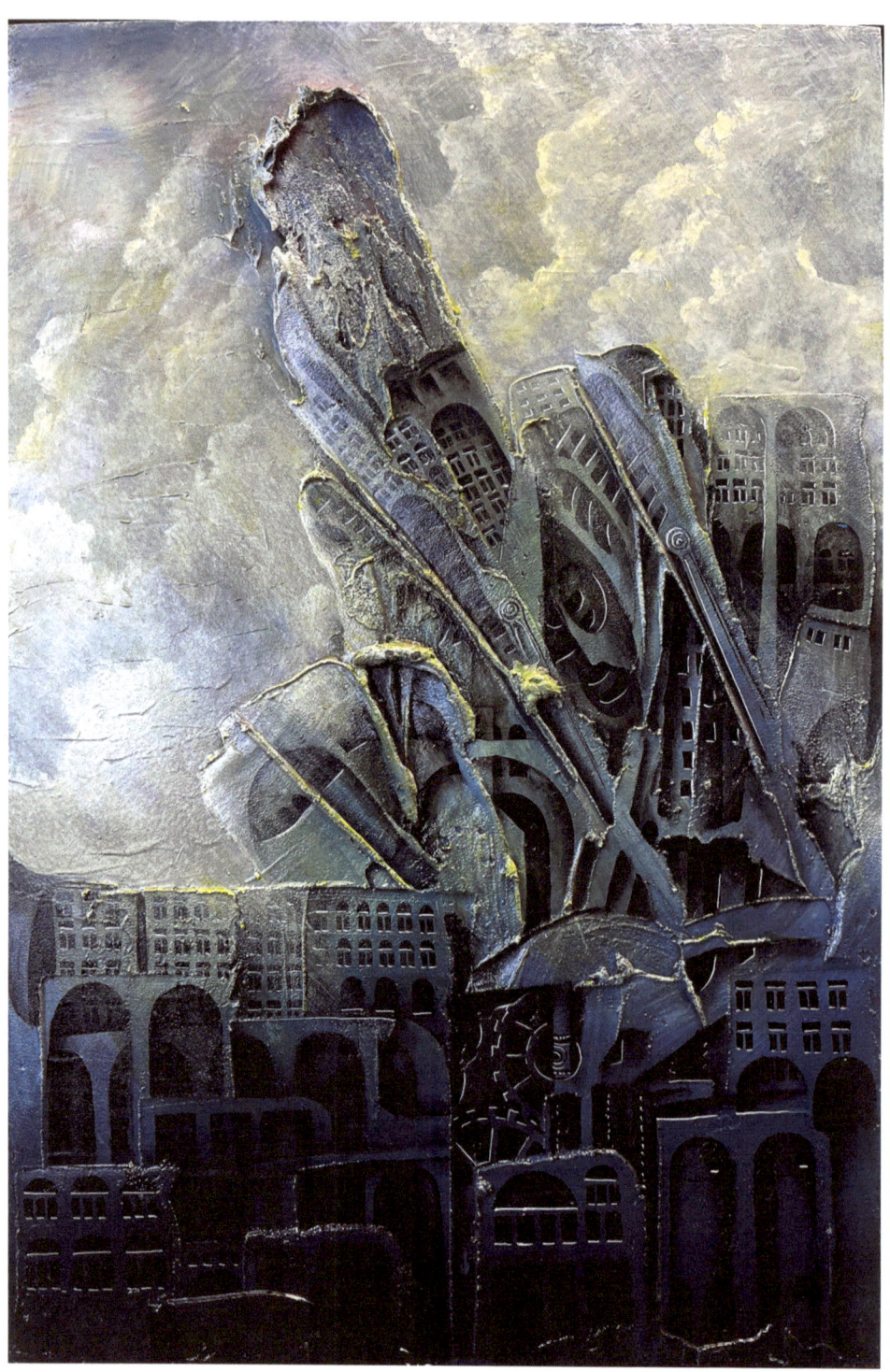

FROZEN IN TIME

the dreams feel more like memories
and I know they were once reality;

Mother Earth wants to share the pain
with every living creature

to re - member
what was once dismenbered.

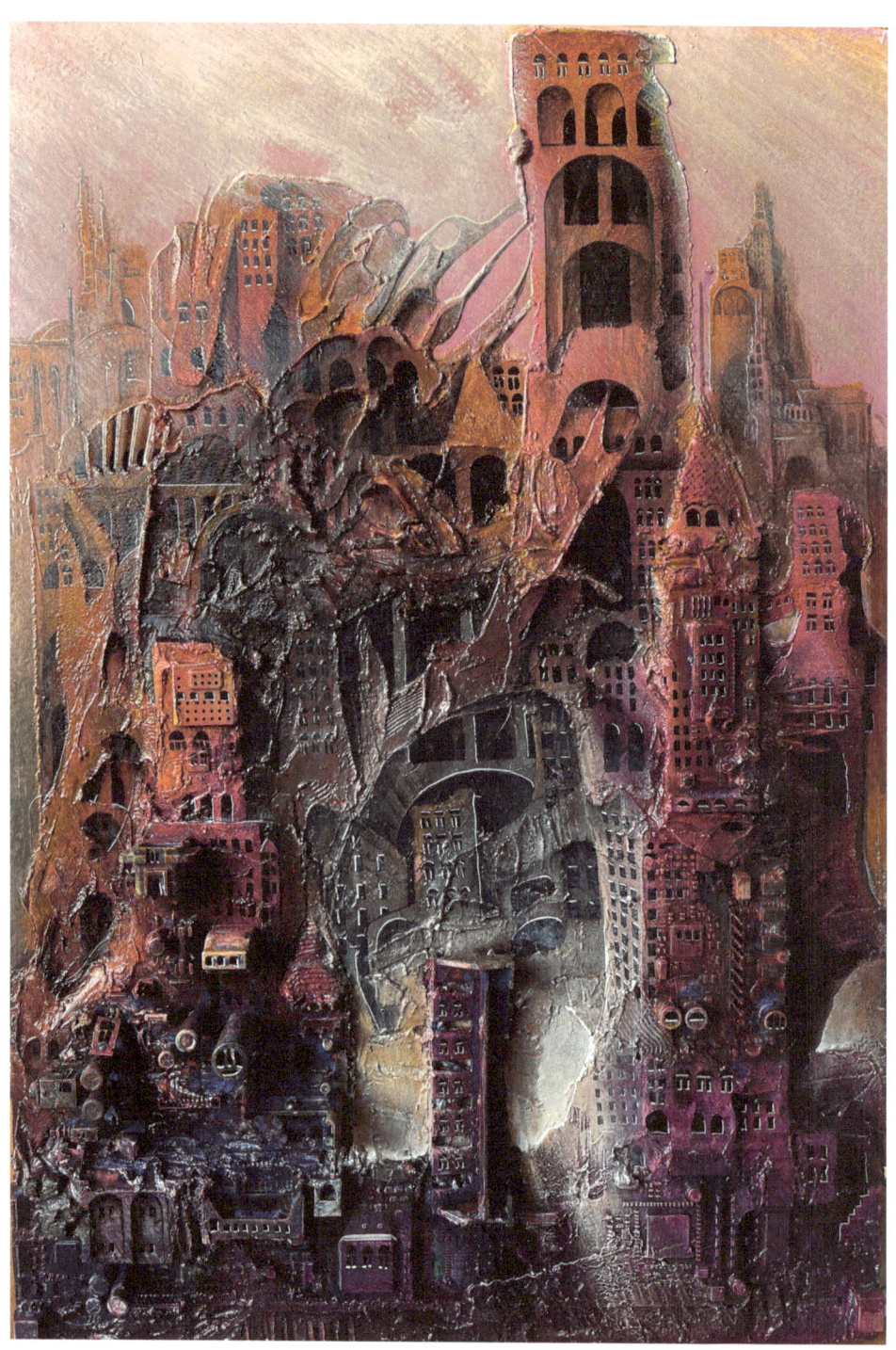

JUST MOMENTS

Moments come and go
holding on to them is painful
since they are not meant to be
owned.
They only are steps to eternity
going up and down
swinging like a pendulum in
time.

And if it is steep climb
or harsh decent,
the view is always spectacular
walking the dream
feeling the fantastic
facing the black sun
that does not blind
in fact, in its darkness
we are the light

light that reveals the inner world
landscape so vivid
that sometimes we close the eyes
to avoid dizziness
to escape
to protect us from paralyzing fear
of losing touch
with our selves

Moments come and go
taking us with them
like boats to distant land

Jessica Gorman

Poetry and storytelling have been a passionate and essential part of my life since childhood. Topics of death, the paranormal, insanity, and the power of personal relationships have been consistently reoccurring themes in my writing; more recently evolving into deeper explorations of the Supernatural and Unseen forces that drive and shape the rhythms of our lives, hearts, behaviors; and our personal journeys to uncover and discover individual meaning and purpose in this life. This project was created during the pandemic as a way to remain connected and spiritually alive during a time of unprecedented global isolation and loneliness. It is my first publication and collaboration; a marriage of my photography and poetry exploring my own intimate journey through Love, Loss, Life, The Universe and the Everything we find in between. I'd like to dedicate this work in Loving Memory of my Father, Mark Gorman, my biggest supporter and fan since I could hold a pen, my hero, and the greatest storyteller I knew. You left this world too soon before I could share this gift with you. This one, and every one that follows, is for you.

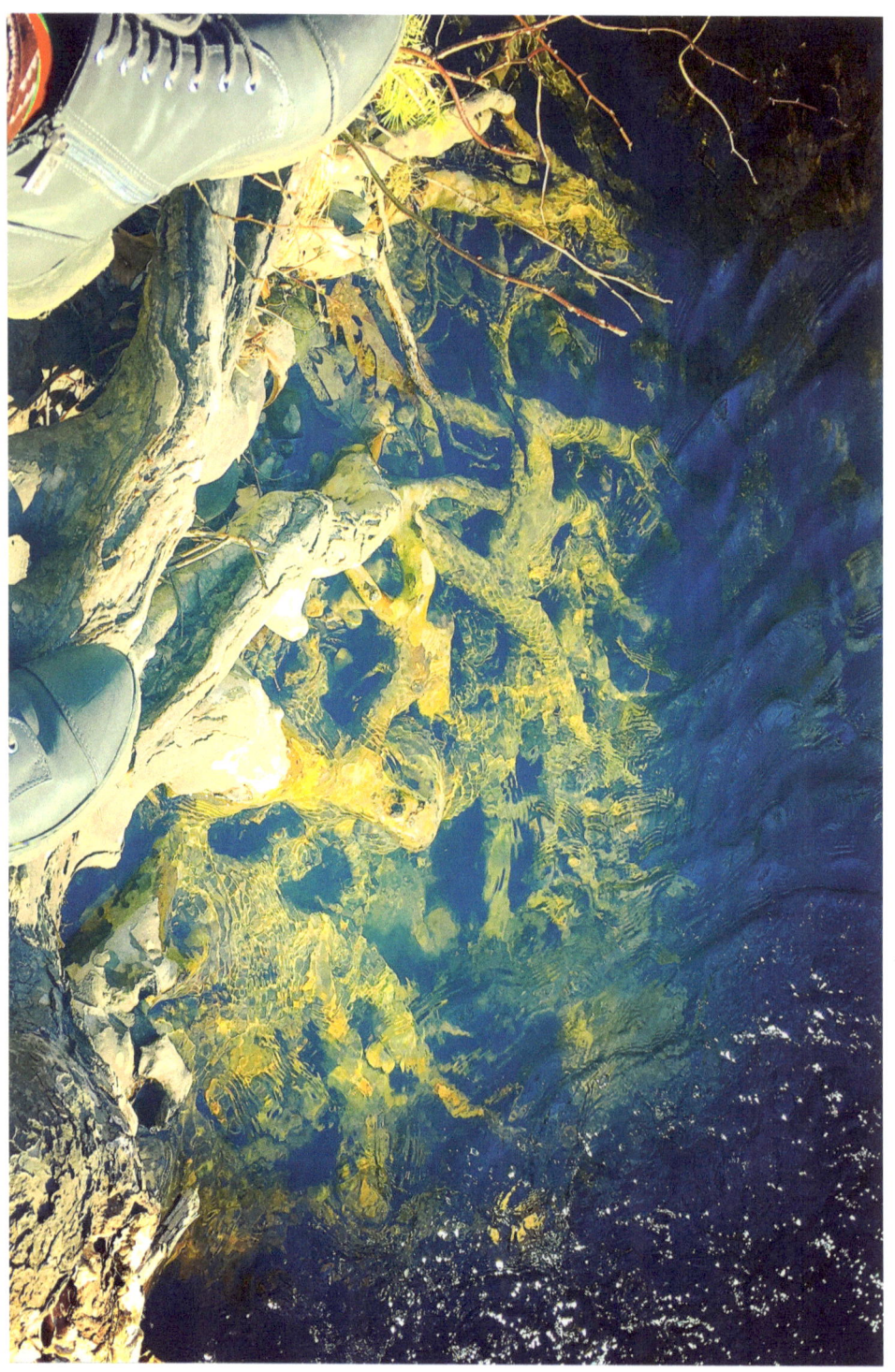

A SHADOW'S KEEP

Where Secrets sleep
but never Lie
Where Wicked lives
and never Dies
A Forest of tendrils
that threaten to strangle
The Light from this World's effervescence…
One must see that in essence
that it is We who hold the key
to the vault underneath
where within lies a map
with our names at the top
the handwriting the same
as our very own.

Way down
At the bottom of
the Darkest Seas
Where our Deepest Troubles
and Wildest Dreams run free
Lies a dark space
An entanglement of roots
Where the only way up to the surface
Is Through

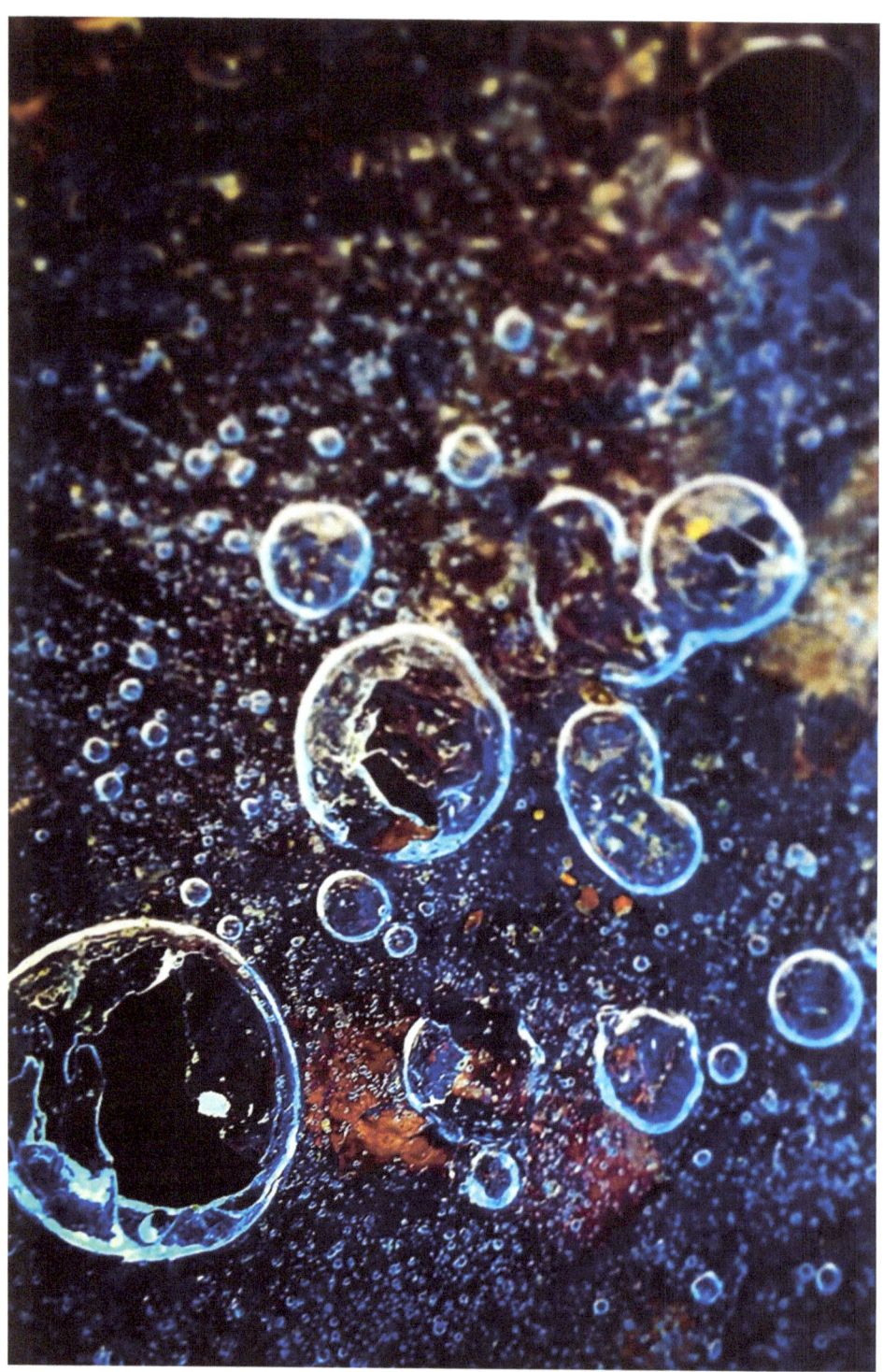

WINDSWEPT DREAMS

A breath of wind
A gentle sigh
Underneath the sky
of an unbroken moon
Where soon
we will offer
to sever the binds
wound round our minds
And send them back
from whence they came,
A place we chose
to walk away
from long ago.

Let us
Bring back the Undead things
born of the Flame of
Older Days
And say no more that
we are not the same
As we sail this sea
of Windswept Dreams
I hope that you'll remember me
when we are Orbs again
and free to Be
as we Are,
A tiny network of Hand Holding Stars

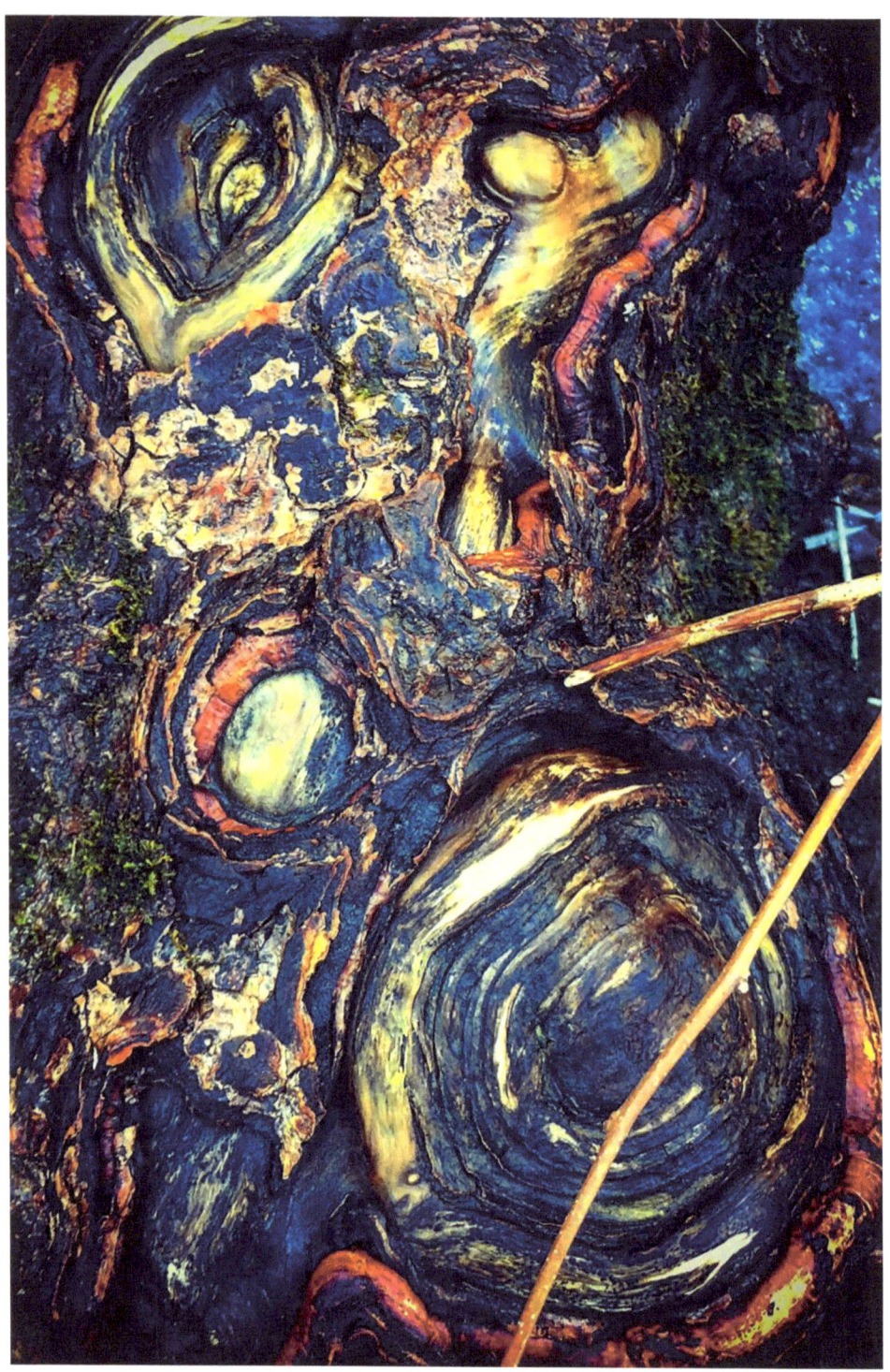

CIRCLES UNSEEN

When it happens again
(It always will)
just know that it is not the same
It cannot be so,
Though it may reek heavily
of the familiar
it is only similar,
ride the wave.

Nostalgia
Revisits
Stories retold
Lessons relearned
It is only
The Absurdity
of our Circles and Cycles
that answer only to Nature,
our Will not considered in this
winding round in scattered patterns
like expanding rings within aging wood,
Etching, engraving an abstract imprint
creating an entire Universe
from our unplanned paths
that become the whorls of
the fingerprint of our unique existence
The beautiful mark
we leave as proof
That we were here

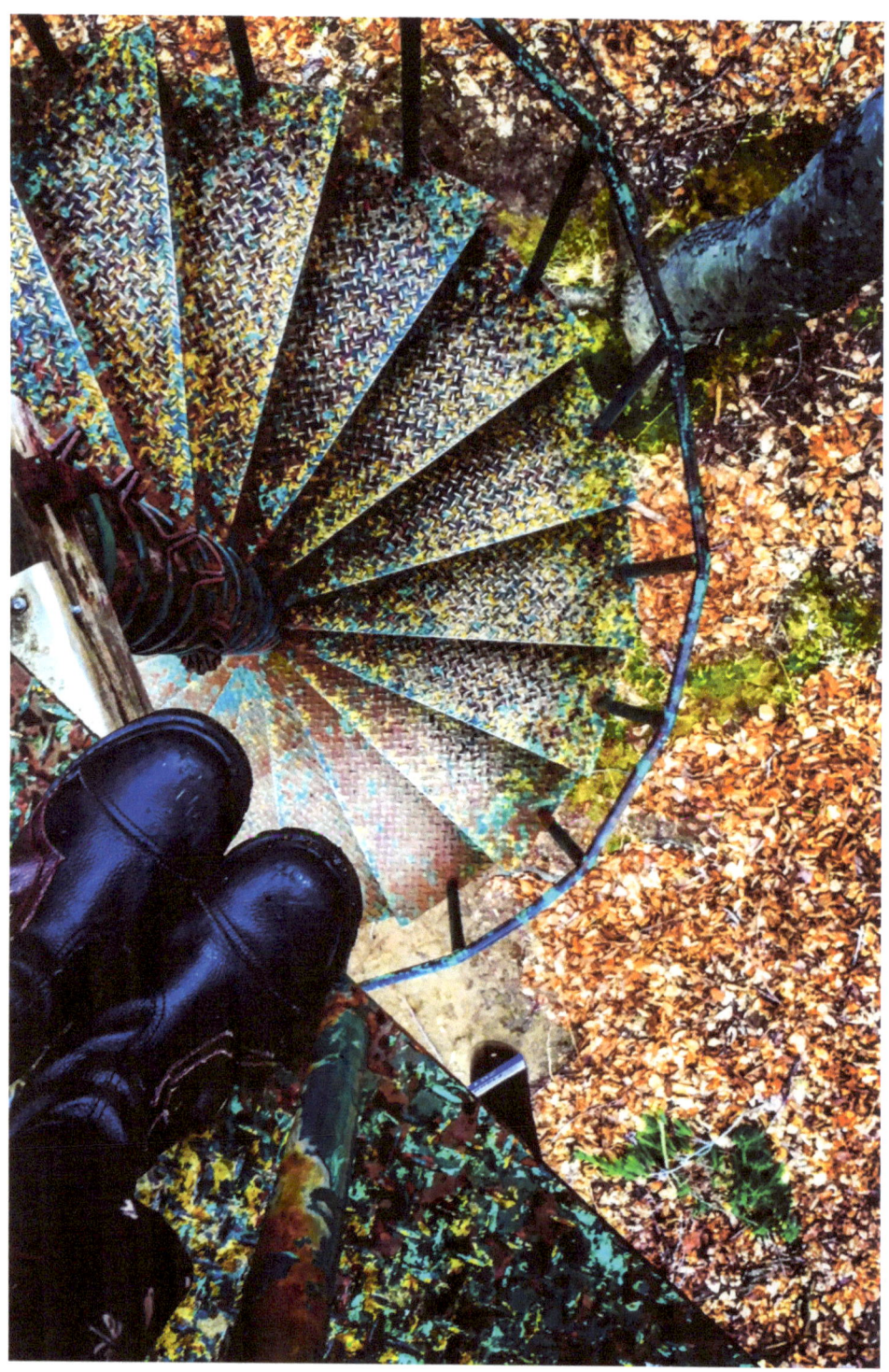

FEAR OF THE FALL; THRILL OF THE JUMP

A fear so deep
so near and dear,
it is easily mistaken as a friend.
Always there,
a Wolf in sheep's clothing
and only knowing this
is hardly an effective consolation
when it bites.
Its venom spreads Despair and Doubt
(((oHmYgodTheresNoWayOUT))))
I will tell you
Madness has a voice
and its Loud.

Always faced with a choice
Reaching out for a hand,
The one I found was my own.
Not so very alone
We looked down at our toes,
at all the IMPOSSIBLES down below,
And they were frightening
but I said
"LETS GO!"

And when we got to the
Bottom
we looked up and saw
that the Terrifying Jump
wasn't a jump after all,
There was always a series of
 steps
(Small and inset)
That aided Me and Myself
in our gentle descent.

I said to Me
I'm glad We Went

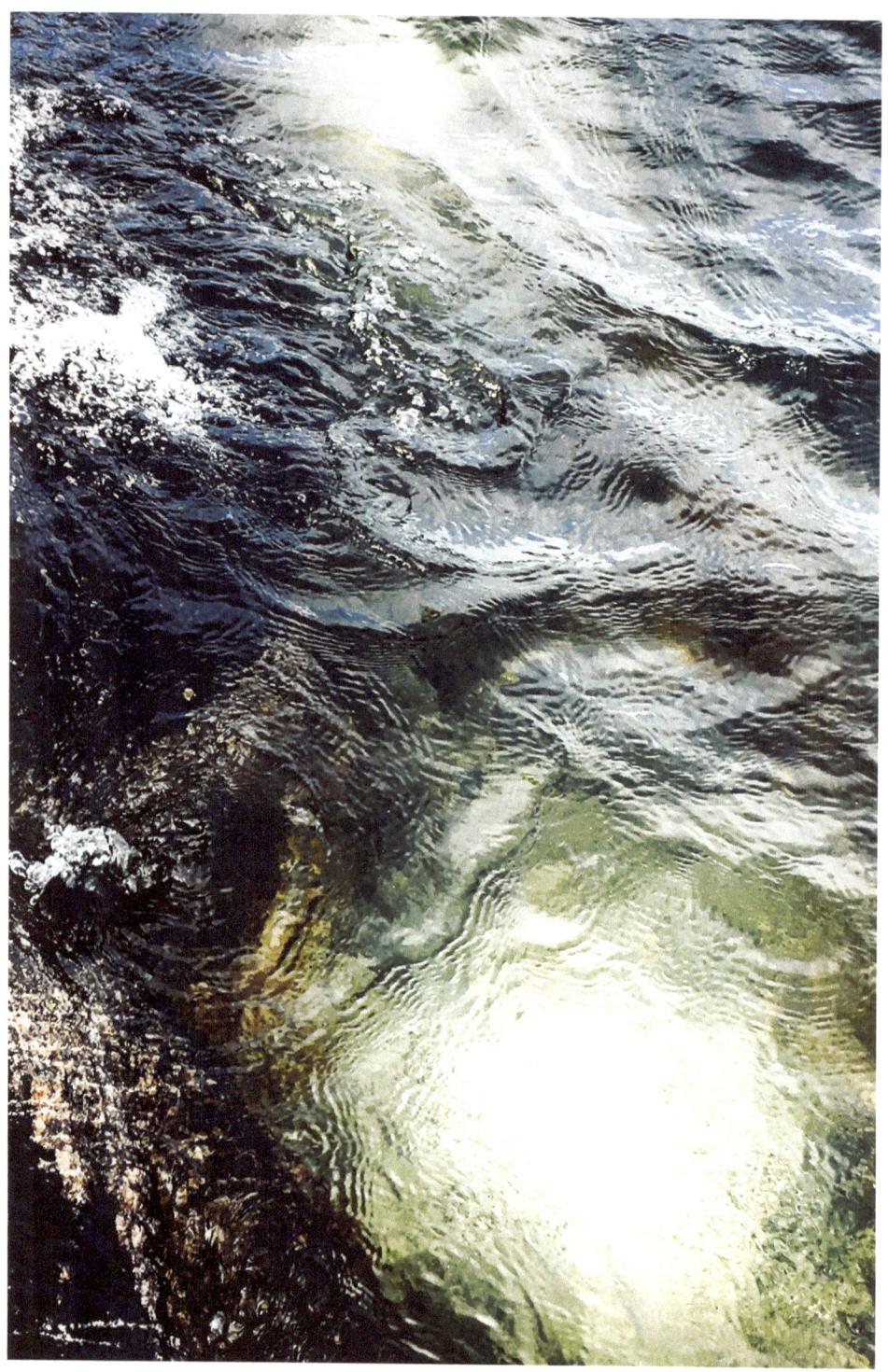

ETERNAL SLEEP

Returned
to the Deep
Set free by
ASleep
I let you go,
in a place that you know.
Now One
with the waters
that beheld you in life
you're a star in a place that exists
beyond skies,
Your stories now echo
beyond the water's edge
Where we will someday
meet again.

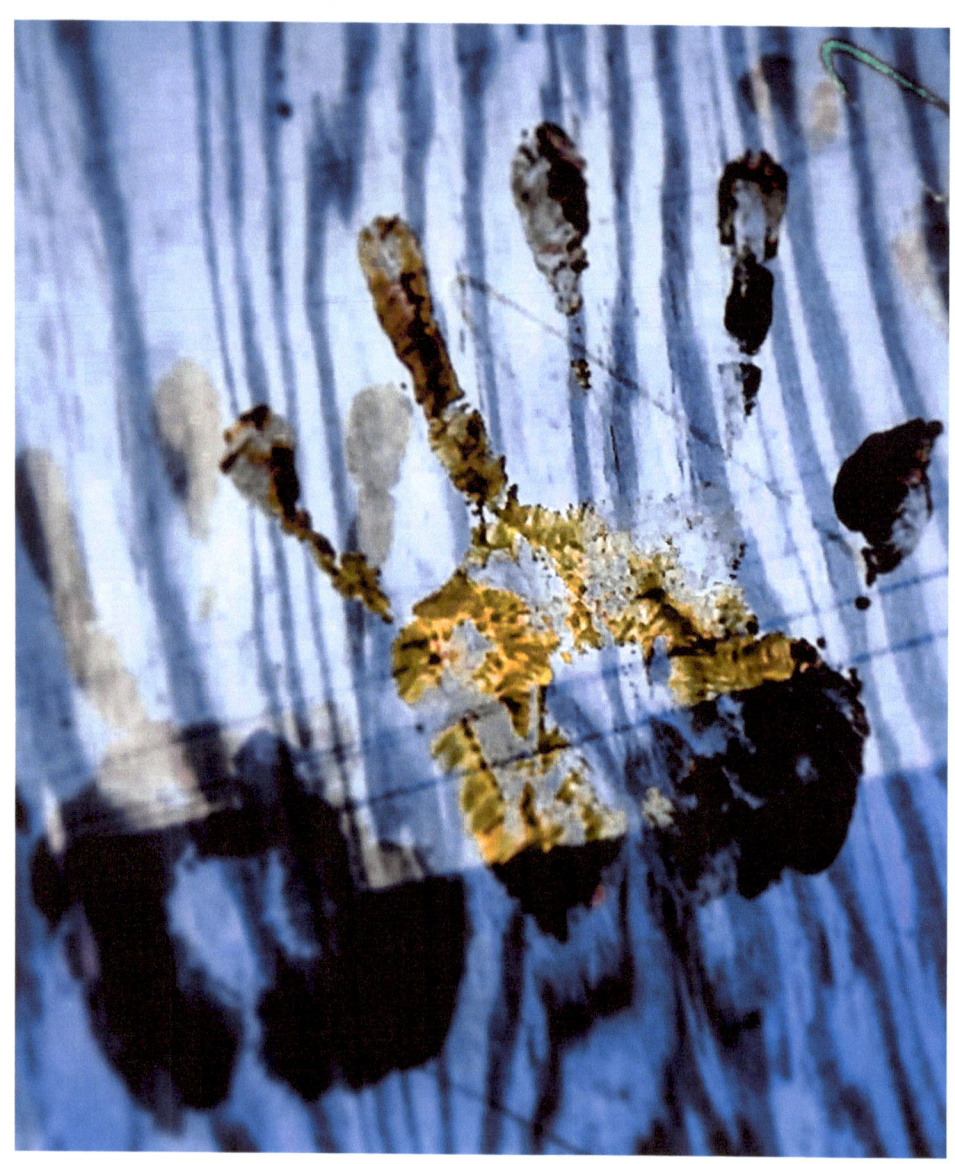

A CHILD'S PLEA

Just out of reach
Your Hand - The Need to feel
it's Life - It's Warmth -
Its COLD
like you
that day
they left you there to wait for me......

And I said
"WHAT ON EARTH ARE YOU STILL DOING HERE!!?"
Swallowed fear with two beers
Raised a cheers "HERE'S TO US!"
to our Final Goodbye.
Some nights, I still try
To reach past the light of the stars
To tear straight through
this mortal Time Space of ours
Till my fingers bleed
With the need
To hear Your voice

Because the last time we met
you mouthed the words "I Love You"
Spelled out S-E-E Y-O-U S-O-O-N
(It was all you could do..)
And for that to be TRUE

now up past the MOON
I must go to find you
I must strain to reach
The Space Beneath
Beyond Between
what can't be seen.
I REACH until I cannot breathe
I cannot SEE just know I NEED
To Get There.....

But
Each time it's the same
As my hand falls away from the window's pane
I see
It's my own palm's reflection
Making two
It isn't You.....

What lies beneath?
A Daughter's plea
To hold her Mother's hand
Once more

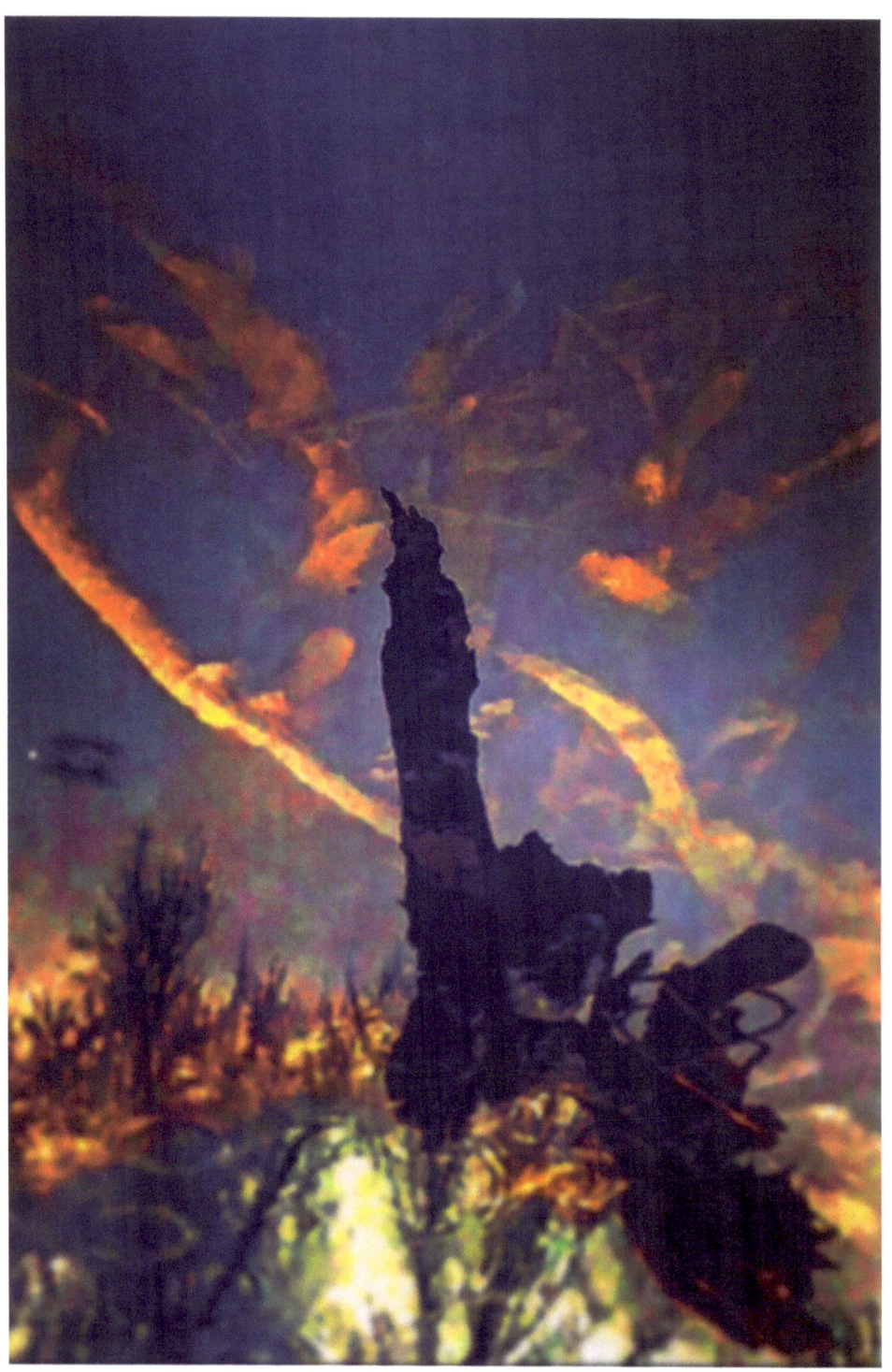

A NIGHTMARE'S SCREAM

Gone...

All gone

I saw It burn......

No one said it would be like this.....

Each last moment a halted breath -
Filled with ashes,
Broken shards held in hands
                      Charred and Sorry
                                just trying in vain........
                                        to just make it
all go back together again......

                What sort of dreams dance in
your head?
                    How do you talk to those
now Dead?
                          How do we maintain
our own Light?
                                What Horrors
keep you up at night?

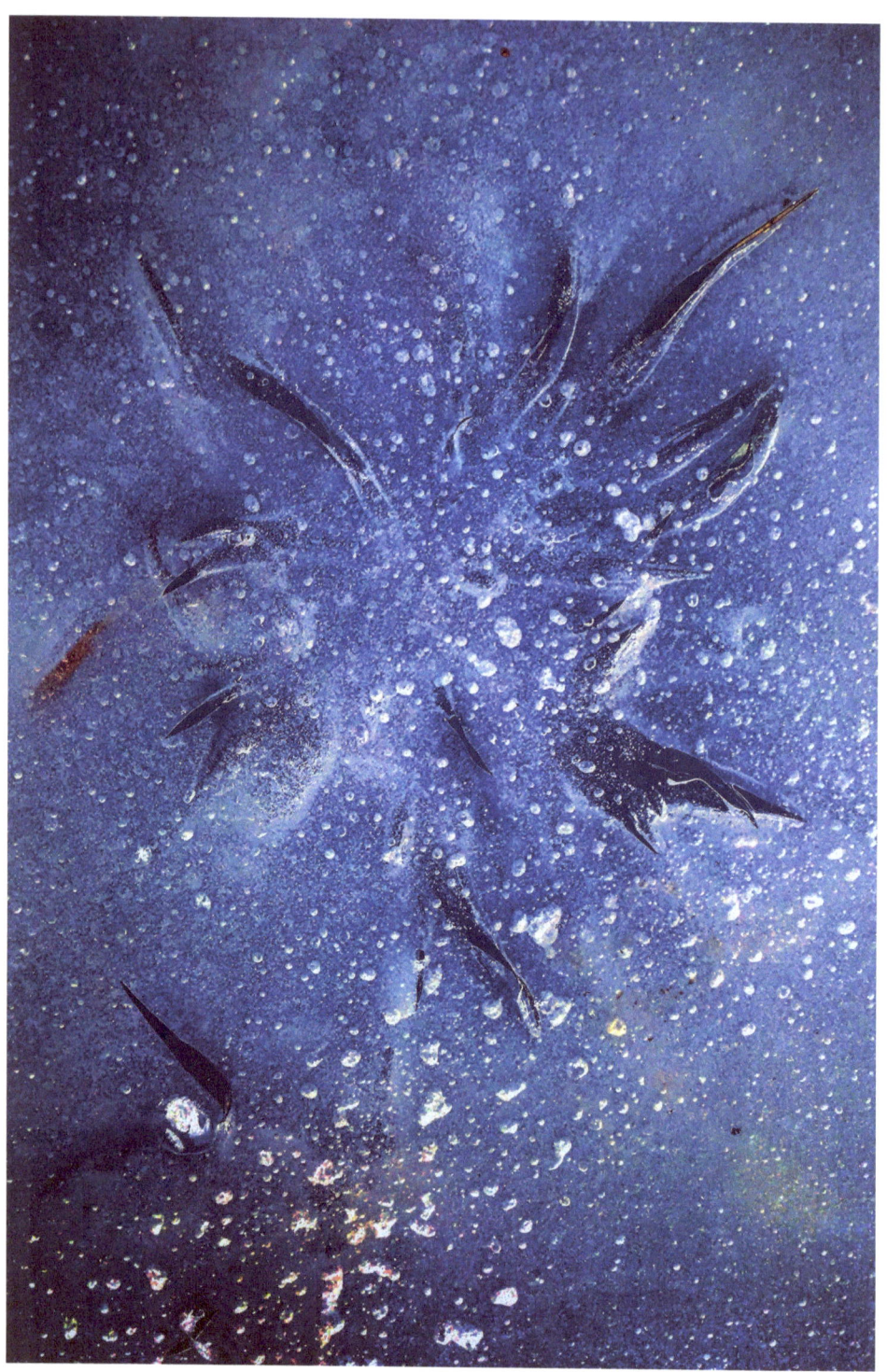

WHEN THE BLOSSOMS FREEZE

What shape
does Authenticity make?
Born to make our own way
through the reeds of Chance we go
Leaving a trail
impressed on this Earth
So specific
Like a snowflake
No Man's crawl is quite alike
We cannot know the shape of our own Deaths
But we can attest
whether we've done our Best
So when Winter comes
and our Flower succumbs
to The Great Freeze
we will leave
A shape
of a Life well lived
Like a flower unfurled
for all to see
The hope for what can beautifully Be

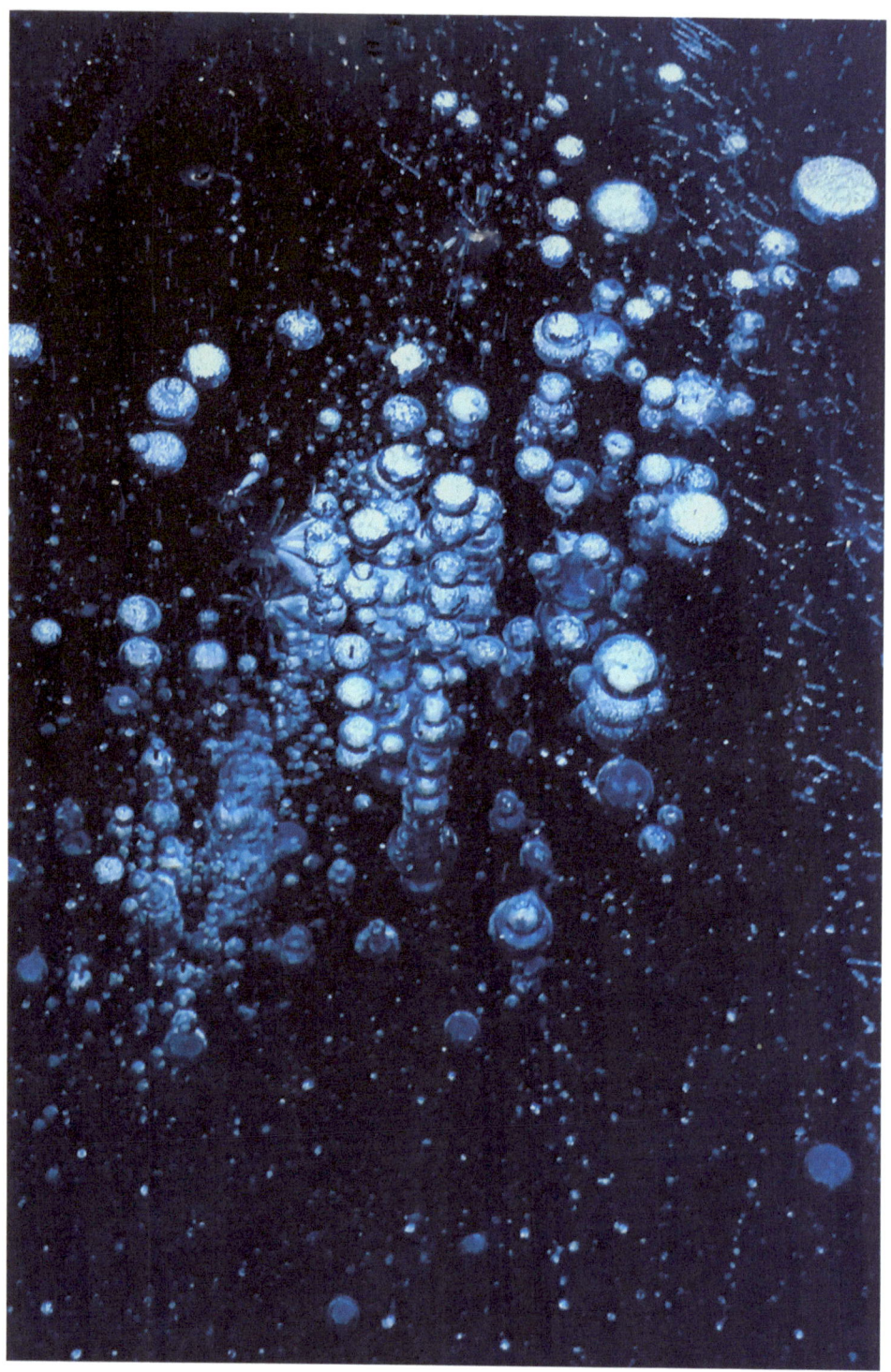

OUR FINAL BREATHS & TESTAMENTS

Just Breathe
They say
Count breaths
like sheep to fall asleep or
to pass through
The Unbearable
To reign in the weep
of an Agonized Cryer

Just Breathe
They say
when the worlds falling down
all around
are the fires set by
Maybes And Should Haves
of Yesterday

Unless it's the End, it's not
They say
and what even is "THE END" anyway?
For tiny Orbs such as us?
Suspended in a cosmic smattering of endless curiosity
Upended from a Time Before
and birthed through the hollows of Earth's floor
Surged forth into Existence by cataclysmic explosions
from deep in the oceans Below
We find ourselves scattered across a great many miles
of Mystery feeling Lost and Alone
Tumbling terrified and awestruck along
on our merry way to Maybe

What awaits us?
What can we expect? Will we explode upon impact?

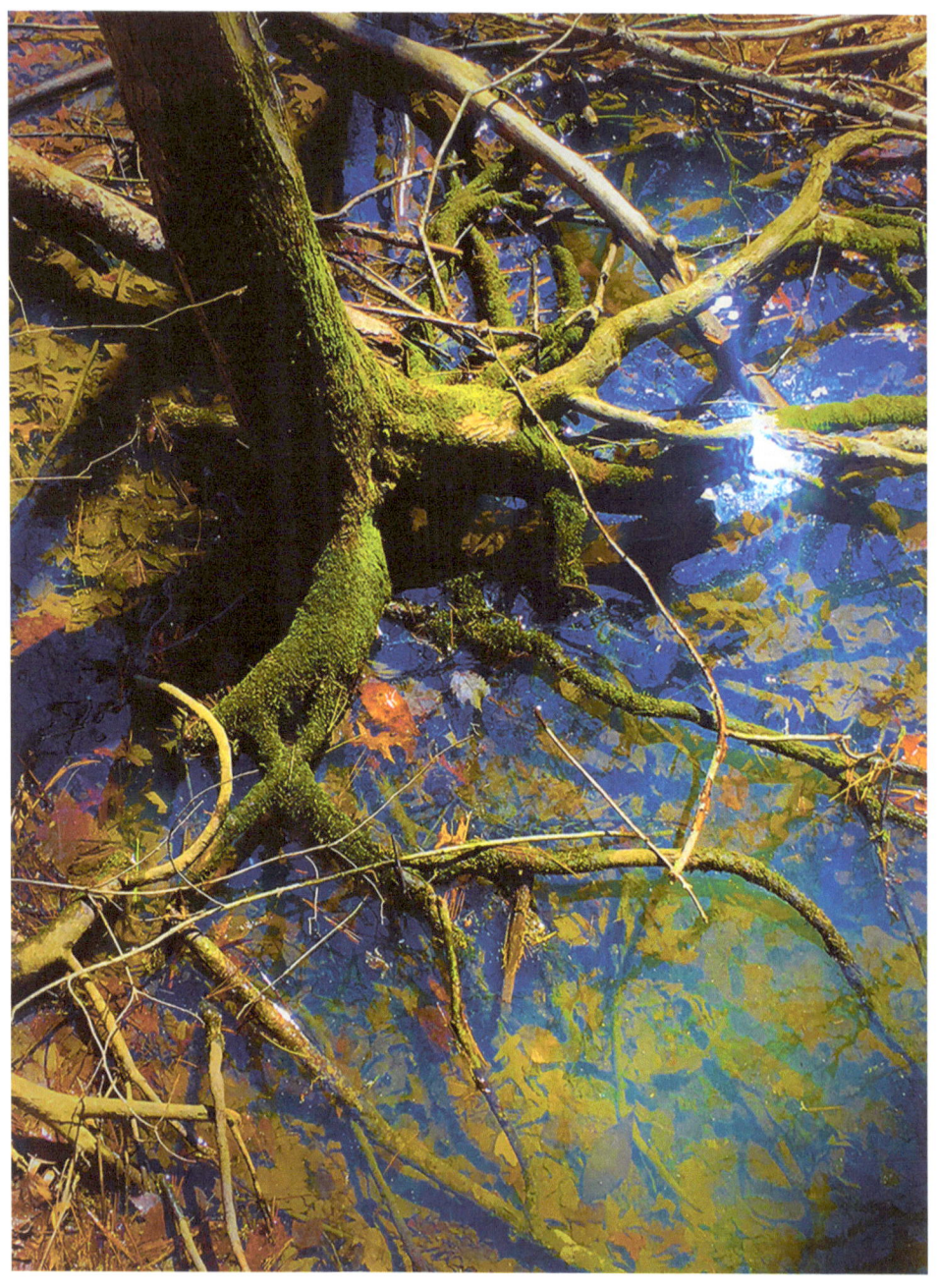

Hit A Great Final End? Or be Born Again
With eyes anew to a world dripping in brilliance
Will we scream our way in as we did into this one?
An Unknown Not To Be Known
we float on towards the surface with no way to
slow pace
past creatures born of Love and War
We rise and gather, like sustenance,
a deeper Understanding of our
Fragility, Stability, Senility
Humanity, Humility,
The Power of Tranquility when the Futility of
Living takes hold round the throats of our Dreams

We Must Build within our Selves
a place of Peace
Release
The Fears that bind and blind
Rewind
the downward spiral back
Relax
Just Breathe
They say
And I find a sense of calm in knowing this,
When Death comes for His only kiss
That of all the lives lived throughout time
I'll be proud to say this
One was Mine

Review: *In Between The Unseen*

By Vitek and Jessica

In Between The Unseen is a luminous collaboration between two artists whose creative partnership was forged within the inspiring community of Gateway City Arts. In a space where nearly every staff member was also a working artist, Vitek and Jessica connected through their shared commitment to GCA's mission: fostering a safe and dynamic environment for all forms of artistic expression.

When the COVID-19 pandemic forced the venue to close for 16 months, the world outside stood still—but inside, creativity continued to unfold. During this time, Vitek and Jessica created a body of work that would become the foundation for their joint exhibit, *What Lies Beneath*, which marked the reopening of GCA's Small Works Gallery in the fall of 2021.

The exhibit, featuring Vitek's paintings and poetry alongside Jessica's photographs and original verse, offered a moving exploration of solitude, resilience, and the unseen emotional landscapes shaped by global upheaval. Its powerful reception inspired the idea for a book—one that would preserve and expand upon the intimate visual and poetic dialogue between the artists.

With the guidance of Paul Richmond of Human Error Publishing, *In Between The Unseen* emerged—a book that not only documents a moment in time, but invites readers into the layered and reflective world created by two voices in harmony. A testament to creative perseverance, this collection is both a record of survival and a celebration of what can be discovered when we dare to look beneath the surface.

www.ingramcontent.com/pod-product-compliance
Lightning Source LLC
Chambersburg PA
CBHW040243220526
45473CB00001B/353